POETRY COLLECTION

BLEEDING RED:
CAMEROON IN BLACK AND WHITE

BILL F. NDI

Langaa Research & Publishing CIG
Mankon, Bamenda

Publisher:
Langaa RPCIG
Langaa Research & Publishing Common Initiative Group
P.O. Box 902 Mankon
Bamenda
North West Region
Cameroon
Langaagrp@gmail.com
www.langaa-rpcig.net

Distributed outside N. America by African Books Collective
orders@africanbookscollective.com
www.africanbookcollective.com

Distributed in N. America by Michigan State University Press
msupress@msu.edu
www.msupress.msu.edu

ISBN: 9956-578-26-6

Dedication

To every well-meaning and suffering Cameroonian

Table of Content

AUTHOR'S NOTE

The pages of this collection speak for themselves. The blood that has bled with freedom yet to come tells the unsavoury tale of my mulling as well as those countless of my compatriots over the state of things in our beloved country. These things just as the country, I would place above all else including life. Conscious of how sensitive the power hungry Cameroonian is, I would he takes his time in reading and appreciating what he/she has done to his/her country as well as what he/she should be doing for his/her country. I have, in this volume included at the end what I call the 'Smattering of Pidgin Verse' for the reading pleasure of every Cameroonian schooled or not. Poetry is for all.

Bill F. NDI

ANTHEM FOR ESSIGANG

O, macaroon covered with poor chicks' feathers
Go sit down and pride yourself in thievery
Like the slums your disgraceful flag shall fly
With your havoc to your name ever true
My father's house that once all tongue could tell
Has now become a house of thieves
So the rest of the world can see
The emblem of the tears of our people

Clan of mbokos, clan of bandits
With death and sadness in our store
Thine be disgrace, thine be great shame
And repudiation for evermore

KAMERUN'S AUGUST VISITOR

When a thief gets into the safety vault
It is never any one's fault
Not even when all is evident
The mission was by Mr President
Ordered just as I did to kill 1985
And to bury 1985
With none seeing me welcome 1986
Whose ghost, in this month of my birth since
Pursues me. And the journey I remember;
Awaiting high school GCE results
Harbouring no thoughts of assaults
And on board a bus from the Tropical Rain Forest
To the Grassfield where rest
I hoped I find,
To my ears the wind
Came chanting of Nyos, Cha and Subum
Where the bomb resounded boom, boom, boom!
And to nature, turned the architect's accusing finger
And when in the future, I wonder,
Will my ears of the truth drink
For all I know if I think
And think properly is I didn't touch the Grassfield
When I was told God's chosen grandsons were in the field,
God indeed has shuttled them there quicker
And faster than would run any duiker
So they could minister care
And mask the tear
For all to delight
And follow the light
The light they threw away from the truth
And none will ever know this in sooth.

THORNY ROSE

Looking at her thorn you smell nothing of a rose
Looking at this Rose, one won't stand to oppose
Her pollens generating allergy
Cannot but push for an allegory
The pink of Cameroon was that of the lobster
How come Cameroon is headed by a gangster?
Such a pink coloured beauty of a rose
In this country takes an overdose
This overdose of a thorn,
Six and twenty years old, has the nation apart torn.
When it started
All would want stated;
The nation got up that fine morning
Surely in autumn not spring
And had lobster for dinner
To embrace the shiny lustre
Singing panegyrics for a November rose
That grew to pierce the nation's heart so close
Leaving many a man
With thoughts of how to unman
And rehabilitate the thorny overdose
Or accompany him to eternal repose.

THE FALL OF BAKASSI

When Bakassi fell, France claiming Cameroon
Nothing did say that would herbusiness maroon.
A lesson our morons refuse to learn from
And would ties project to heights top in form
As the French her glass of wine savour
Poor cam marooned ions bleed in labour
Relations between states: interdependence.
Yet, the dependents joy with independence
While their providers dream and dream by a river
From which they cannot a bream take, never ever!
Cameroon, Cameroon, forty-eight years running
Cameroon, Cameroon, forty-eight years crawling;
Sit up and stagger
For you're no toddler
Not just this pen would want to see you
But those you've made poor need to know too
So, this pen may go to sleep
Letting their hearts like frogs leap
And land anywhere in the land safe
And worrying not to be enslaved
As they've known all these years
They have spent shedding tears
You refused to wipe not being brave
For all you are is France's knave!

ENCOUNTERS

Up for the show,
Everywhere I go,
I do tell them from Cameroon I hail
And with "a great soccer team" I am hailed
And I would soccer returned stolen flag
Of corruption politicians won't take back
Making every victory in this game theirs
Instead of wiping off the poor their tears
Winning in every game but looking after the poor
And when this game they shall win, poets' pens will praises pour
And their thirst for them will forever be quenched
As will the poor their imposed pains have entrenched.

PSEUDO-PSEUDO EPHOR

We must be dead drunk to always doff our hat
To such a rogue whose every move is so bad!
Moil! Moil! Well known sing song in Cameroon
Where the people's sweat, the ephor's saloon
Keeps cool to his comfort and joys
Of piecing the nation as toys
And how else could he play this game
Being twice shadow of his lame name
Pseudo-pseudo ephor
Makes and makes no effort
To lift his little finger and support
The discomfort; that will steal his comfort,
His birth right not trite
To see all their rite
Perform and have the nation's heart beat
For every threat to become his treat;
Applauded by those behind the mask of his mask
He reigns absolutely and would none anything ask
Now, my people, why sing a song so sad?
Are we deaf to hear it displease the heart?

OUR SUCCESS

Countries end up!
Mine in a cup!
For the best we do is abdominal
Lifting of the cup in way practical
To a fowl after quenching her thirst
Mechanical sports in which we're first

French tip, *pot de vin*
Cameroon tip, vain
Potamology finding one with water
But that big river overflowing with beer
Play the game, shake your skin
And you are a great kin

In this land where water must taste bitter
The bitterer the water the better
In benumbing the bitterness by foreman
Devoid of regard, brought to bear on man
Go round the world such numbness
You'd never find with success!

HERITAGE

When she was born with hopes people revelled
And trusted her to a nurse from the Sahel
This nurse his luck for years tried, two and twenty
At the end his vision he lost twenty/twenty
Sung was liberty
To infinity
When November came to Cameroon in 1982
She was a young woman only twenty-two
Fresh and rich with buxom youthfulness
Scaring away thoughts of the dryness
November could bring to milking her dry
At forty-eight none would recognise her
In the prime of motherhood
This her childless widowhood
A thorny heritage from the groom
1982 had stuffed with gloom
For this beauty whose beauty
Does underlie jealousy.

POPE OF CAMSIMA

Adventurers as he in these pranks indulge,
Yesternight was Germany, today Asia, and tomorrow Africa;
Intelligently thou fly the world over.
Bat! Bittering the sugared pills.

Laity thee applaud,
Ulcer of social injustice in scale's name
Addled-brain, this month (November) you brought.
Past glories of the Sahel all gone?

DREDGING MOKOLO MARKET

Extinguishers never their job did
Yesterday STAMATIADES I watched
To ashes go down
Yet, we had extinguishers
A week after, they could
On market ants, their job do
And under their weight shivered Mokolo.
Yes, right they might have been
For the sake of market "development",
But, the miteless…!
Top on their agenda, malnutrition,
At school doors knocks September
With school requirements yearned.
Yet, mothers' cocoyams crushed,
Our boxes they crushed.
Under the canopy of uniform
Peacemakers, millions
Swashbucklingly took,
And to keep us off, water, they sprayed.
The Lilliputian General Gaston I saw,
Up he went, down he came
In that way to be in the dark read,
While at gun war brink
He does nothing but shrink
Now sending his boys at us
He swaggers away
After ordering itchy water on us
For us to go body scratching.
Why not order their job
Using water to fight fire
Than use her on market ants
Crushing with bulldozer their merchandise?
Yet, we nurse hopes for global health,
Extermination of poverty, malnutrition….

ASSASSINATING DEMOCRACY (INSURGENCE)

Place: Bamenda
Day: 26th of may
Year: 1990
And six of ours
Went down!
Standing their grounds
And for their convictions
And gunned down
By the forces of regression.
I know not what official History say of them!
But, May, the month we screamed out
"Mayday!"
In quest for liberation from the chains of tyranny
Deserves that attention worthy of any Victory.

Martyrs are these six
In this nation where no dead is a hero
For what we live for is the here and now
A less conducive one for a penman!
Yet, I long for that day this Mayday
Shall itself fit into our official commemorations!
Our Martyrs' Mayday
Victory over dictacracy!

GORJI GUANO

Draped was the sun's face,
His glimpse of it vibrated his larynx
His pen embraced the paper we yearned
And the flesh of the leafy castle this tore:
Our head's. he then his shackles commanded
As that of Lilliput for Gulliver's.
His hounds crooked their knees,
Behind BARS lashed
Him, though one, called at this Association.
Thermis' cadaver met he there
To respire thanks to her reproaches,
Queen of the Isles, thank U! Gorji
I now know the inner colour of the sun's face.

THE REAL GUANO

Dropped always by a Grassfield bird;
This one like Gorji
Stood up voicing
Strangeness: Pluralism!
Which needed blood bath
And six hurried to the park and went off.
So it came!
Retarder now claims
To be the promoter,
Relinquishing guano
And barring him from lying on the farm.
But one thing shines like the sun.
He emerged like a stubborn
Stunted oak tree in a storm
Tenaciously negating fall
Chant: "Non Idiots
Join Our Hands Now
For resourceful Unison
Not Discouraging Intellectualism."

A thing abhorred by the prince
Never heeding our cry
But seeking reconciliation
For a crime unknown!
Guano is the only fertilizer
For you plants…!

FROM THEN TO DATE

I remember,
At three
Galloping from neighbouring
My eyes hosted refugees
Nigeria into the Cameroons
Like cows from a thunder stricken herd.
Their hooves sang like the locomotive
Killing me with fright
By night
Dreaming of embracing monsters
To hook on my mother's
Chest.
In my ears whispered:
Dissipating my fears, Parents
"They are plagued by an ill."
The horses did confirm.
My ears drank a myriad saga about same wave,
I grew up, of the war I read,
Jostling me to pondering the devil
And my gun triggered,
Brain mother of that evil
Aimed Western arm merchants
Goading Biafra's slaughter
And burial
In Nigeria
As canapé to economic prowess
Now questing power-tricks
To push one Nigeria
Into many Nigeria
With an umbrella of oneness
"Southerners we are."

(54)

As a kid, I thought masks were only worn by masquerades,
And/or idiots and cowards
That coloured my Cameroonian childhood,
Growing up, I read of clowns
And had them replace the childhood masquerades
And thought they best fitted them! No! Mistake!
The politicians they fit Best!
And like my childhood ones,
Politicians use these to coerce fellow human beings

(95)

The beauty of roses,
The beauty of roses,
Is in their never going by the appellations:
African, European, Asian, American,
Nor do they identify with such
Accolades as Cameroonian, Dutch,
French, English, or German.
In line with the language of emotions
They are not in terms of origin expressed
Yet, the sausage making side of humans
Between One World and One Mankind stands

CAMEROON 2008 ROBBER IN THE NATION

Walking out of northern winter
Approaching austral winter
The changing tide of time
Intones a new chime
And up rises everyone ready for the show
But Mbivondo would everything slow
Freezing the nation
Cuddling division
In oneness,
The death bearer's madness.
His edict like a morning rose
Unfolds and all take like junkies on overdose
In the house where the knaves applaud
Him life sentence lord
Bringing wonder when death in his sentence
Abridges his life pretence
Lord he
Shall be
For life shan't stop
'Coz he did rob.

GAB ARTISTS OF AFRICA

Were obdurate Gabe to rule Cameroon
And treat every national like a moron
Mortgaging the forest and oil for thirty years,
An overwhelming YES
His acclamation would be
His sweetness likened to honey
And he would his dirty shoes sheen
On the red carpet the White House keeps clean!
None would cry foul
As none hears cry a fowl
From Cameroon chased, hunted and killed
When free is the underground to be drilled:
Shell
Unleashes a bombshell;
Sundown
Brings nations down;
Elf
Bedevils the self,
In short the multinationals
Must new rationales
Instil:
Africa needs to be still
Not with Gabes at the head
For they deprive of bread
Both nationals
'N Multinationals;
To cut a long story short
Not 'coz of word, the poet is short:
The latter should the last word
Have and the former their ward.

BIRTHDAY PARTY (2008)

Gold Rich Ritchie splashes
Half billion for his miss
Bang, it hits the news for all
Down under, only a call
                            To Cameroon
                            No macaroon
                            A text to Rina
                    Void of a spinner
                        No chocolate,
                        No accolade,
   All greeted without bands
                            With two hands
Welcomed with reckless abandon
Its real worth in imperial ton!
Owning no stones
Worth attracting she who through stones
Does real substances read
Bent on seeing nothing greed
Not even when the sea the sand washes
Washing it away from the beaches
With beachcombers left to fast
Without hopes they'll have breakfast.

TOXIC WASTE AT HOME

With his crew, he screws the nation
They exhale carbon dioxide
And inhale everything oxygen
These are all platitudes!
But the truth you don't know
About everybody in this nation
Breathing just carbon dioxide;
Bought with trees from which came oxygen
Denying all attributes
And letting waves to grow;
Grow waves and sweep,
Sweep, sweep, sweep,
Sweep with you this toxic waste at home
And leave home clean as the pope's in Rome

YEARS GONE BY

Four hundred years have gone by
Since James the first told his lie
By right, God on earth he stood in stead
Reason why his son was executed
For a crime he didn't commit
For, before there was none to thwart it.

In Africa four hundred years after,
One coveting the foothills of Sabga
From the Americas came
Discovering here that game
He could play and finding allies
In the new James, his name Pol, lies.

That game they will play but here we are
Waiting to be fed full to their char
For our Pol has become Saul
Who does think now with no soul
And doesn't see how much harm is being done
Like a priest giving hope we'll be reborn.

With time passing by
Our river they dry
And we must not wait to mourn her
For with their lies they will choke her
A sight we would not want to see
Yet, from which we must not flee

We have come this far in this struggle
Beautiful attempt to keep trouble
At the bay with native Ambassibay
A dance that thrills us by night and by day
As years have gone by all isn't the same;
So, why must we shy from telling Pol SHAME?

SLEEPING FAKO

Thanks for taking pity
In your sleep on slippery
Siblings of ours East of the Mungo
For they know not your anger can flow
Flow to drown their jewel on the littoral
Sleep Fako sleep and wait for our refusal
To carry their shit for long
They've made us smell all along.

In their ignorance, lords they themselves
See with piles of bank notes stacked on shelves
Priding they own us and our land
And calling us Anglos, our brand
Hoping this in us crushes resilience
The cornerstone to our thundery silence
One that has lit in them such fright
Like Saos' voice setting birds aflight

Fako cough not in your sleep
Fako snore not in your sleep
But forget us not the day we say no
For then we would want to see you blow
Blowing up those on us placing shit
To carry for they think us unfit…
But in the horror of your volcano
We'll paddle on your lava our canoe.

And leave for freedom land
Away from Mimboland
And from your spring we shall drink
So shall siblings this fact blink
That your years of dormancy
Did not grant Legitimacy
To shitocratic reign
But grounding a restrain…!

BABY AMBAZONIA

Was from time immemorial born
Was through time and age grown
Was of the Federal Republic lured
Was of the united Republic deterred
And by the La République killed
And in death tied to the skilled
Assassin since in hiding gone
By his wall of soldiers and canon
Shielded
By the whole wide world greeted.
Need not emphasise a true story
For all know and none does worry.
Poor Baby Ambasonia
From your ashes rebirth is so near
For my belief in this myth
Has nothing of a heath.

C J'S CATTLE MARKET

The herder from the north drove his cattle
Seeking a market south by which he did settle!
Super Paquita, Yaounde Stock Market
Did welcome a drunk and a coquette
And they did choose to run
And steal from the nation the fun
Invading her entrails
With the storm of hails
Cleansing the future generation
With backs against reformation;
Look not back in anger
But rage of a cyclone no prayer
Would stall from sweeping that son of a gun
And his hussy like a skunk
Perfuming the nation
Suffocating respiration
Welcome the desire to shroud
Their sun with the thickest cloud
So, none can smell the moron's breath
Needing checks on its strength
In the warren they hide in.
Then shall future generation win
The cattle market of its coquette
Cleansed, stopping the drunk's racket
Through which fun was stolen
'Coz fun and nation bond can't be broken
And this strife must not relent
Till happiness, emotions and passions vent
Spreading across the land from the southern forest
North to the Sahel, East and the Grassfields West.

A PLACE I CALLED HOME

I used to know a place called home
And when summer came it was our Rome
Where by the door Papa would his arms stretch
And the blessings he poured had no stench

But one day the phone rang
Bringing news bigger than the big bang
He heeded a call from far above
Turning down all our hopes and love

And to bit him farewell, we got home
Home was not home
Rome was far and gone
And stolen was the Sun

The Sun that our summers did brighten
Echoed news of how frighten
The nation once was as news came
The dictacrat washed down the drain, fame.

Yet, I knew home was still home
For sweet, sweet mother built a honeycomb
From the waves that did dry our tears
'N America the gates flooded with tears & fears

Tears and fears, in arrears we had
Not just in war torn Iraq and Chad;
Today, go not there with this in mind
Go not there hoping for a find

For heart and head of home having stopped
Of joys and hopes we are robbed;
And beyond the still buildings some call home
Nowhere near papal bliss in Rome;
Life is a million light years.

But closer than close to fears and tears
With only tyrants to set the rules
Hoping to work to death the willing mules

In this once upon a time place called home
The boys in green the streets roam
Where parents would not they're grown
And they in them keep the calm away blown

Where Peace and military are antithetic
For the latter birthed a bomb atomic;
Yet, our soldiers here keep the Peace
By hook or by crook and breaking one apiece.

Away from that coxcomb
Order home like hair with a comb
Letting just wind touch the scalp
But beating like flax the soldier's slap.

A war mongering lord his rule set
And De Gaulle might have said:
"Get ready for war to attain Peace."
So, the reverse of courtship for peace.

And away from home, the globe, our village
Has the waves set on rage
Stealing the peace the kid I was knew
But, won't stop my dream of home anew!

By mom and dad supported
By that ring disappointed
And by the dictatcrat and war mongrel robbed
Anguish and despair for the idyll are bobbed!

Countrymen, willing mules, those laws
Into you forced like tiger claws

Into its prey forced, 'bide not by
Contain pains with no cry!

A cry, tyrants won't even hear
Or in which they'd only read fear
Displayed by weak and feeble mules cowering
For not the left and right knowing

Then shall tyrants see need for growing
To feed peace loving mules their blessing
And home shall be home sweet as honeycomb
Sweet honeycomb sweeter than bliss in Rome.

And gone has been that ring
That news of bigger big bang did bring
And farewell we'll bid tyranny
To have a phoney free story.

Once again, this place will be home
Where children feel the smoothness of chrome
And dreamers will freely dream
And mornings will joy on faces beam

And why won't home be home once again
When pains mules stood are now a gain?
And once again the sun will for all shine
Leaving none not even the blind.

05-13/07/08
Last 6 stanzas composed 19/09/08

BLOOD 'TWIXT GREEN & YELLOW

When the waves wash off our coast
Not far from the Chariot of God, our boast
Spitting flames golden yellow
Telling of forebears' Sorrow
In Victoria near Cape Limbo
In our twisted tongue, Limbe
We dream the flames will be out

When the waves have come and gone
We wake up to see nothing undone
Not even the blood stain 'twixt green and yellow
On the flag flapping as the waves goad us follow
Not as our parents did with the République
That burnt, killed & buried Federal Republic
Where Paul as Jo before does pout.

MARE PROVIDERS

Fascination and awe grace repugnance for a lion
Be him in or out of his dominion
His characteristic strength to kill,
And he dexterously does with a thrill
Sending home a chill down the spine of the sleeper
Frozen by thoughts of terror provider proper
Found in lion kings like Suharto,
Polpot, Paul Biya, Momo, Nguesso, Bongo, Sese-seko…
The one and only thing none will stand to look,
A thing to make a nation puke
For the king is a lion in rage
Wanting in and mimicking lions' courage
Desolately in the marshes
Where he for the preys searches.

THE NEW SAUL

My baby ears savoured with pleasure
The Bible story of Paul who did treasure
Killing when he was Saul
The like of the crowned soul
In my part of the jungle
Who his way does bungle
To hugging that knight of evil
And chopping our fabric like a weevil.
And touched was that knight
By the light
In the broad light of day
And in darkness he did stay
A night times three
Then was set free.
In the light, our crowned Paul
Did start but was dull
And by this, rushed into darkness
Where he did to greed and heartlessness
Take
And like cake
Did enjoy them
And without a problem…?
Remembering how he did come to the head
I recall all sat under a baobab tree shed
And from above parachuted by Redman
Came our headman
Like the book they used to promote gore
That since became, here, the lore!
Redman, Redman as a guise thou didst unseat a king
And with this one to justice thou won't bring
And I quest why?
And wonder where the truth does lie!
When he worse has done to his kind
As thou to thine did, though they're kind;
Doth thou on these grounds do embrace him?

Or art thou afraid of the fat he'll leave thee slim?
If thou art the light in defence of the defenceless
Here thou hast a case of helplessness
To defend and set crowned Saul on the path
Saul treaded on here on earth to avoid a second wrath.
Saul to Paul I love
This Paul with Saul hand in glove
I deplore
And do, the world to unseat him, implore.

ETOUDI ROYAL RAT

The royal rat
In the royal rat
Warren
Does warrant
Our journey out
And would never come out
To face us
But would chant to us
Tunes of royal persecution
And one of royal persuasion
To his lackeys
Forgetting we cats without keys
Will at the gates, patiently wait
Until late
For his Royal Lowness
With astute unholiness
A life prisoner
Himself makes sooner
To keep his tunes alive
And find himself in our hive
We shall dance
We shall dance
Here!
Here! Here!
And go into a trance!
Not in France
Where he would refuge
Seek to avoid the ire of our deluge.

GHOST LION

Defying the senses known to Hellene,
Stalking the muddy streets of Melen
The muddy Ring Road
The muddy Bamenda-Ekok Road
The muddy Bertoua-Yakadouma Road
The dusty Maroua-Banyo Road
This sleazy
      Shiny
            Flighty
                  Filthy
Ghost, a living tyrant
Goliath the giant
Mbivondo
      Of Ewondo
Adorns posts and trees
And in his name weary travellers forfeit fees
And in turn sunken into the ghostly hallow feet
Before the Ghost Lion deprives them of all feed!

LANGSTON & EYE

Hearing Langston sing America
I too would I did sing Africa
But following the saying charity begins at home
In my dream and wish I would I were sitting on a dome
To sing not Africa but Cameroon
A lovely country that mankind maroons.

Hardly was Langston counted with the stock
And never did he count himself short of luck
Cameroon my case in point would rather we were cows
Or muted subjects willingly receiving arrows
But Langston as well I call them what they are
Mother fuckers with no nous of the three Rs.

ETHICAL CRIMINAL

He called himself a poet
Knowing his days were numbered
He shamelessly quintupled his shame.
What a shame!

When wind brought home his death
Instantly knowing not, pity rained
Before coming to learn of his game
Faking everything he ever did claim

His death for sure, he didn't fake.
Yet his life and his death did justice cheat
Leaving all those trapped in his game maimed
Mol, Mol, Mol all fake dead or alive nothing has remained

Consciously he left that 'E' out of his name
A letter to have defined the spirit in him concealed
What other spirit could it be but that of a blemish
With criminal contamination acts, devilish!

Though humans shouldn't judge
How can one face an act so horrendous?
Acts and life of lies leave none unmoved
And all would have it disapproved

As the world should his masters
From them he his trade learned
As the nation coffers they empty to fill theirs
And joining their crew he put on their feathers.

TROPICAL JOLT

If you think the winter sun so cold
I'll send you to Cameroon for a jolt
Wherein our heads have us bribe to be slaves
Against which their knaves keep us in the caves

Sealed with the nation's biggest bolt
Freedom attempt draws thunderbolt
From the salves saluting sheepish head
For only sane minds must their blood shed

To feed the ego of Narcissus in his mirror
Oblivious to digging himself a burial furrow
For when our summer sun sends the chill
We see our head kill many with skill

Knowing on the big ones he can lean
For they care not our nation grew lean
Upon emptying its fat to run their engines
Even if this was by one man drunk on gin

Cooking his brain dead to human sorrow
Killing his thinking of a tomorrow
Were this not enough to jolt you
Then gas chambers give you no clue

In which case misery makes no history
As the promise to make poverty
Growing in strength under such heads
Who refuge find in northern sheds.

GOOD OLD LADY LIBERTY

O, Bamenda from Station Ranges
You breathlessly take one through the ages
With country scenes of movies worthy
The prettiest dame our heads turned ugly
With drunkenness teeming in their heads
Buzzing like a swam in their bonnet
Maddening them to redden our tarmac
With the blood of freedom! This hellish pack
Would kill before it grows, in your sons
Cameroon would rather rob of sun
Buried in their forest of darkness,
Rain forest seat of great unkindness
Whose palatial load does weigh heavy
With your fields by this absurdity
Crippled in the desert their forest
Bears for no one to ever know rest
And responsive you are responsive
Shaking off with the wind, deeds of thieves
Who would stomp and stomp on freedom's grave
Forgetting freedom's ghost the most brave
Like liberty's grass from her ashes
Like phoenix reborn from its ashes
So Bamenda flash the freedom flag
That will turn tyranny into rags
For your dead sons to smile
In the grave where they pile
Unforgotten
You begotten
Staying not clear drawing weds poetry
Like our fingers with clay in pottery.

SOUP KINGDOM

Here in bitter leaf soup kingdom
Our people's will has been benumbed
Stinger king Bee spreads his tentacles
Which reach and rid our receptacles
Of the sweetness of bitter leaf soup
A fit not to us any new scoop

Bitter King Beer on his drunken throne
Crushes and kills all hopes of the drone
Staying away from the bitterness
Of king's stiffness here in readiness
To sap the bones of all marrows
King can't kill our dream of the morrows

The pink of our prawn will kiss the rose
That will satisfaction really dose
Against the greedy sweet soup container
Emptier happy we own no coffer
His favourite kill our satisfaction
Kills with a kiss the rosy nation

Cameroon prawn pink bitter leaf soup
For which all in this nation stoop
Save us who've tasted the bitterness
The king crafted out of greediness
And shoved down our throats delightfully
And we now on scripts throw up wholly.

DUSTY WITH THE RAINS

They're such a kind lot
Suffering patient lot
In cruel hands of a slut
Though an intelligent lot
Quickly losing it
Hearing money's shit

Money is neither alpha
Nor is money omega
Take money for either, your business
Woefully falls to dark unkindness
Ignoring people may dream and dream
Cash flows and drowns fish screaming down stream

Cameroon is contended too dusty
With the rains and with dryness muddy
Telling why natives dance without music
Unmoved with her gripping spell of magic
Magic these conductors wields with their wand
Polluting the brains blind to understand

Now we would paint our brains grey
Conductors wish make us bray
With our backs against their thought
They have no choice but to snort
And our children will sleep peacefully
Pack of wolves went home disgracefully

ONCE A NATION OF GIANTS

Nation of Sao, people know not
These giants of yore reduced to nuts
Cracked by monkey from the rain forest
For this new nation know not 'tis blessed
To use the differences of strength to build
And not selectively to make a guild

Elsewhere of yore they called that mafia
In Cameroon, of Essingang we hear
The puppet masters running the show
Pulling the strings for these giants to slow
Down, depleted of energy
Where there's great need for synergy.

Giants, harden your nutty shell
They'll crack you not nor you sell
On your feet standing up tall
Not long before their great fall
From their great wall of ignorance
From which they project importance

With neither colour, taste nor feel and sound
But stinking misery to which you are bound
With shackles you will like Agonistes break
And rattle for the whole country to shake
Off the yoke of enslavement deceiver
Has so far used to dress you black griever

Essigang dark art artists club's
Joy's to see the poor drum with clubs
Not to send out the sweet drum beat
But cries that push them in a feat
As the clubs fall, the poor cry off their heads
So do their tears fill cups to oil heads' beards

Fuzzy drowsy look that beams and shines
With such joy that puts criers' lives on lines
To killing ancestral vocation of crying
Offering this once upon a time realm just dying
Only the future would dig and bring to life
Even when the years in millions have passed five.

WEDDING DAY

Miss Cameroon had a dozen
Bridesmaids and groomsmen chosen
It was November sixth the wedding day
Curse for which the nation still does pay
And the men ushered her out with all our dream of bloom
Into such reality painting pictures of gloom
Sneaking in this scary and ghostly hydra
Who has bittered our bitterness bitterer
Selling our nation to the West
'N freedom we cry in our nest.

QUIET, ALMOST SAD

Being a favourite son of the West
He rules this country just like pest
Let Cameroon sing as they play
Playing for her love to delay
A union made in who knows where
Needs not be forced down here and there
For freedom's sake, fall prison walls
Exhibiting their lack of balls
Flagging shameful flag of horror
Boiling steam our guts with furore
Like Samson's to put on some dread
And save this suffering lot from death
Freezing life quiet and sad almost
In pitch darkness by their lamp post
The West have rosily painted bright
In vain attempt to shun our plight.

UNPACKING CAMEROON

Hanno discovered her
Chariot of God was her
Name Hanno ignored
Above her hell soared
With its angel bee yah
Driving chariot that far
From God Hanno won't recognise
And would now want to rebaptise
Her blaze eternal one from hell
With glowing presidents that smell
Hunting human noses to the grave
When they all would have loved to have rave.

LORD OF GREED

All Bitter you are free
Too stand tall like a tree,
To lift your shoulders till it licks heaven's arse
But not to treat the honest man as an ass.

In being rich you yourself pride
We'd tell you that's foolish pride
For your wealth can't put ones like us asunder
Rather change your name from bitter to better.

In your ocean of wealth you swim
Besides you a waterless river limp

As you hoard your water
Claiming to be better

When our waterless bed does feed the poor
Telling you to down the drain your greed pour
Will you tell Cameroon that greatness
In your lexicon means greediness?

Our unborn child would love to hear
Of true greatness of the poor taking care:
Where oceans do fill the rivers that feed the poor
Making true greatness, one that shall never go sour.

But before I pick the oars
I would like to raise my brows:
If your soldiers protect you and not the weak
How can I say you are better than the weak?

Lord of Greed
From weak breed
Assert strength and come out
Be welcomed by a crowd

Cheering up your courage
Not jeering in a rage
By your greed embittered
Please have this registered!

If not you should step aside
Else we'd get you out of sight
With our pens bleeding to drown you in your ocean of wealth
All the nation is asking Lord of Greed is some good health.

A SONG FOR SHEPHERDS

Cameroon, teach your shepherds
A song to sing as they herd
Were they good to you they should be happy
Not like drunks in hiding and unhappy
Taking you their herd for a dumpster
Failing to shine your way like a star
Their falls from grace like all tyrants
Attracts them only woes not grants
In their illusions of might to which they cling
So shall reality dawn on them like bee sting
But with songs of victory over poverty
History they make will live to be such a beauty!

FORCED ...LOCK

It was nineteen sixty
Years have since passed near fifty
When we got married
With joy we're carried
Before the celebrant united nations
They swore to witness us on all occasions
And then you cheated on me
Before these torn nations that be
When at the door knocks divorce
Arm merchants desiring force
Behind you run
Supplying you gun
Their dirty game is not my business
But you won't push me into a mess
Not with your tongue nor sword
Winner I shall be my word
Let's recall the facts with dates
Starting with card games as baits
On 11 February you deceived me,
In 72 May 20 you tricked me
Today, I am the enemy
Whereas you are slimy
Wanting to tear down our home
You shall always hear me groan
Given that my request is not unreasonable
And I am not an object so undesirable.

THE SAD CASE

The Portuguese had their feast of prawns
By the river they named that of prawns
Which became a curse for my country,
A name which to carry is heavy
Giving Cameroon a hump on her back
With a saying regarding a prawn's back :

Circumstances forced the prawn's back hump
And the Francophone in our throat the lump
Inviting surgical intervention
Needing nothing divine intervention
To keep lump off our guts
Calling for one with real guts.

Sad is this case, for the problem
Is not the hump but their anthem
In practice eating like canker the fabric
Making Cameroon *The Corrupt République*
With us dreamers crying for two
'Coz in the Federation we're like two

United by common interest not greed
Through which their *La République* makes us bleed
The last drop of blood in the name of the father-
Land where the distance to everything is farther
From the pretence of union we once tried;
Carrying *La République* for which we're tired.

MY BROTHER PHONEY

Who does it better than you do?
By day you would hoot as owls do!
I don't heap you blames!
You do name me names!

I would make you shame!
For claiming such fame!
Anglo-con!
Anglo-fun!

These of me you make!
Would your shit I take!
Like frog swell up with Francophonie
Blind to your deeds as Franco-phoney

I won't want to be funny here
As your claim to be high up there,
High up there in your folly
Defeating Franco's folly

He dragged Cervantes' Spain into gore
Which today you have dragged to our door
Would you take a mirror and have good look
Then tell me to keep furore off my book

Brother phoney
Must be Looney
Were you to dare this upon
All what you've already done

What else can we embrace but furry
Though you would the world from you curry
Favour with such gestures as would knaves
But take this home: slay thoughts of the caves
A master behaves!

He never enslaves!
He serves his subjects
Well, not between decks.

PEACEFUL CAMEROON

One old man came to me in Melbourne
Curiously he asked where I was born
I answered him Cameroon
He shouted, "What a moron!

Never heard of it, it must be peaceful! "
I quickly corrected: "with prisons full!"
That's why we know peace in her four walls
'Coz all progressive thoughts our leader stalls.

His word is the law…
He's got tiger claw(s)
Long live peaceful Cameroon!
Let yourself known to morons!

A peaceful country with a head
Whose wish is to see all were dead
As he fancies graveyard silence
For him to enjoy opulence.

THE PROMISE

The sun rises in Bertoua with promises
And majestic strides to sweep away losses
Little knowing in Mvog Meka it will fall prey
To pitch darkness long in wait to make sun pay
For such generosity embracing poor and rich
When for the latter sun's V. D. is for the rich
Hostage the sun shall never see Mungo's West
The whole world knows darkness do in the West nests
But pitch darkness taking sun hostage in the centre
Stretches hair strands and makes heart bitter;
The king of darkness in his palace
With such bright smile on his face
Smirking like a ghoul happy misery's claws
In the nation and in the books of laws
The promises the sun made must die
Mvog Meka darkness thinks it a lie
But unchain, we must unchain innocence
Taken hostage by this king: mad and incensed
Married to drunken spree and delirium
Which have taken up all in his cranium
But not our dreams of bright sunshine
We'll fish out of darkness with a line.

SMATTERINGS OF PIDGIN VERSE

CHOP CHAIR
(Thank Choir for Tabenken.)

For Bamenda
We bin tanap far
When Papapol bin chop chair
Yi come for show we chair
Yi come sey yi don bring we shawa
We gree sey na trutrue shawa,
Dat one whey we Papa for up
Don put hand on top.
Spear grass grow for we foot
As we bin di think sey na good thing for stay put
Wait sey make de blessing
Come from dat shawa, we start di sing
Year dem come di pass
And then we see sey yi bin look we na like jackass
Since for we Mbe dem
Papapol yi one bin pass all dem
Dem carry yi go enter Ngumba house
Leave yi for carry all juju for dey go for yi house.
We Mbe dem don loss their voice
Like that ants dem whey bin loss their voice
After dem bin drink strong cough merecine
Today na we dey meng bicos we no get merecine.

CONTREE PIPOLE

Ma contree pipole
Na tie heart pipole
Sense dem get am
Suffer dem di see am
But dem sabi lose sense
For hear sey moni na nonsense

Moni no bin don start something
No bin ye go cam finish something
If you want follow na moni na you sabi
Some man bin enter nyongo sey ye no sabi
Sey na just dream whey di fool pipole
Make dem give chop for nyongo pipole

When moni enter like shit and sand sand
Dem start for high up make we call dem grand
When pipole no look their smelling shit moni
Craze go enter their head drink all di moni
Dem go run go for Oku, Babungo or Mbonge
When small better no follow tori go don badje

Dem bin sey tori sweet tif man laf for banda
When ye badje for Etoudi palace, na wa
With Essingang mafia whey dem di cry for wia blood
Send their sand-sand-boy with their khaki for carry rod
Whey dem go booh we whetam like sey we bin snake dem
Essingang Pipole forget sey na we make king dem

For give their brother for nyongo pipole
As dem think sey moni go buy pipole
Make we sing wia samba
Make we dance wia mbaya
Make dem know sey moni na wia shit
If for dem na ye go buy dem meat

TATANGUMBA AND NCHINDA

Lie lie no fine
Man yi heart no di fine
Na true
Na true
Tatangumba
Tatangumba
A like for know one thing!
You fit tell me that thing?
Yes, Nchinda boy!
Yes, Nchinda boy!
Who lie?
Who lie?
That Mbeh for Etoudi bitter!
Why you no go show yi ginger?
You don fear na only die
Take fear go wear clothes for lie
Weting you go tell your grand pekin?
You fool all man for this world go clean?
A take my eye see bad thing
Ask god for gi we fine king
Since Mbeh di tif tif pass rat
Only come out na like bat
For night make we no see yi
One day moon go show we yi.

PAPA NGANDO YI MIMBA FOR CAMELUN
*Translated into Pidgin from the French, 19/02/09

Papa Ngando bin sabi lukot mutuari
Na all whey yi bin sabi do
Again yi bin di nak we tori
For die pipole whey dem di waka
Yi bin sabi see dem for road them for capitale
For side for Obili and Melen whey yi bin dey
The plaba come pass Ngando yi sey:
One die Anglophone na two die pipole dem
For Camelun if dem dey alive dem don die
No bi for sika sey dem want am
Na oda whey come from up
No bi from heaven, but from palace
Like dey one from up mop for tong
Bad thing no fine for talk
Anglophone for Camelun yi chuku chuku trouble
Na so whey Ngando bin see Camelun
A go like for sabi yi mimba today
For dis one whey dem don troway am for hole
Make yi shut up or talk fransi for gi laf
Gi laf for sara yi ninga
Whey yi di fear reserve bench
Whey Anglophone sidon for dey di wait yi tam
Kang kpwe, yi know sey that power na grong own
Only crishman go sey make some man drink solu water
Even de man whey we don troway am for desert.
But dis contree na Anglophone yi own too!